A CRITICAL STUDY OF R.K. NARAYAN'S SWAMI AND FRIENDS AND THE GUIDE

A CRITICAL STUDY OF R.K. NARAYAN'S
Swami and Friends and The Guide

Ruby Roy

KALPAZ

ISBN: 978-93-5128-042-2
Price: ₹ 90

First Published, 2014

Published by

Kalpaz Publications
C-30, Satyawati Nagar,
Delhi-110052
Ph. : 9212142040
E-mail: kalpaz@hotmail.com

Laser Typesetting : Sanya Computers, Delhi.
Printed at : G. Print Process, Delhi

Cataloging in Publication Data—DK

Courtesy: D.K. Agencies (P) Ltd. <docinfo@dkagencies.com>

Roy, Ruby

A critical study of R.K. Narayan's Swami and friends and The guide / Ruby Roy.

pages ; cm

Includes bibliographical references.

ISBN 9789351280422

1. Narayan, R. K., 1906-2001. Swami and friends. 2. Narayan, R. K., 1906-2001. Guide. 3. Malgudi (India : Imaginary place) 4. India—In literature. I. Title.

DDC 823.914 23

Contents

Preface

R.K. Narayan is one of the major writers in Indo-Anglican fiction. He does not preach, just reflects the reality of India. He is a pure artist. He is neither a social reformer, nor a spiritualist, nor a comic writer. He is an observer of life as it appears to him. His works are neither purely tragic, nor purely comic. It is the mixture of the two. He has faith in domestic harmony and a peaceful world.

Narayan is considered originator of regional novel in Indian English Literature. The imaginative region of Malgudi is the domain of Narayan's imagination. Wordsworth created the district *Lake* in his poetry as Thomas Hardy immortalised Wessex in his fiction. In the same way, Narayan's Malgudi although fictional is more real than any place in India. His characters are the true children of Malgudi. His protagonists depict self-journey from innocence to experience and eventually to wisdom. His plots and characters are inseparable. His works reveal his comic vision of life through irony and paradox. Narayan has excellent command over language and uses it as a medium of story telling in lucid, simple and unaffected manner.

Narayan did not follow the European style of story writing, but bears affinities with American short story writer, O Henry. His stories always end with a surprise. He is a skillful narrator of factual and human scenes. His narration is simple, direct and pointed.

Narayan's *Swami and Friends* introduces us to Narayan's beloved fictional town of Malgudi, where ten year old Swaminathan's excitement about his country's initial stirrings for independence competes with his obsession for cricket and all other things British. Written during British rule, this novel brings colonial India into intimate focus through the narrative gifts of this master of literary realism.

Narayan's matured novel *The Guide* shows us the life of a common man called Raju who has an ordinary childhood, an extra-ordinary love affair, a parasitic life which extends to his term in jail, then his role of a *Sanyasi*, sacrificing himself for villagers and his spiritual awakening. Like a phoenix, Raju annihilates the past and recreates himself.

This book is a modest attempt on my part to highlight certain critical aspects of R.K. Narayan's novel *Swami and Friends* and the popular novel *The Guide.*

I may never sufficiently express my gratitude to honourable Principal Sir Dr. Satendra Kumar Joshi, Satyawati (Evening) for his constant encouragement and support.

I must thank with all my heart my Ph.D. Supervisor Dr Smt Manjari Agrawal and my mentor Dr R.K. Agrawal, Professor and Ex-Head, Department of English (Dr B.R. Ambedkar University, Agra) for their constant guidance.

Last but not the least, I must mention that my father Shri Shalil Roy, my mother Smt Anima Roy and my brother Shomor Roy encouraged me constantly to write my first book and also that they stood as the greatest source of inspiration to me through the entire period of my work.

1 Swami: Post-Colonial *Bildungsroman*

Over the past decade of literary criticism, with literatures in English from countries such as India, Nigeria, Kenya and with literature in English by multilingual, multicultural minorities, such as the U.S. Hispanics and Britain's Asians taking centre stage, the theory of post-colonial literature has gained prominence. It includes all those authors writing after colonial rule or literatures coming after the end of British colonisation. Thus certain features of post colonial novel emerged. Any novel which was created in the language of the colonisers but with an effort to vary that language to express the local culture. These novels expressed a turn towards indigenousness away from the moment of culture contact. Also, such novels displayed pride in their indigenous cultures. Often the hero or heroine of the post colonial novel comes to this knowledge through a journey, especially one linked with the growing up process.

The German literary tradition defines the novel of growing up and coming to an awareness as *bildungsroman.* Martin Swales, defines *Bildungsroman* as highly self-reflective novel, one in which the problem of the *bildung,* of personal growth, is enacted in the narrator's discursive self-understanding rather than in the events which the hero experiences. He talks about the thematic possibilities of the *bildungsroman* focused around adolescent flux and change. Goethe used this genre in his novel *Wilhelm Meister* for nationalistic and class analysis; thus this genre never got dislodged from its prestigious position. Swales also noted that the English novel of adolescence (Thomas Hardy, Charles Dickens, etc.) was essentially concerned to find a certain practical accommodations between the hero and the social world around him.

On the other hand, the American *bildungsroman* as defined in R.W.S. Lewis's *The American Adam,* defined Americanness in the new world and reflected the passage of new world innocence to knowledge through tragedy. According to Lewis:

> The American myth saw life and history as just beginning. It described the world as starting up again under fresh initiative, in a divinely granted second chance for the human race after the first chance had been so disastrously fumbled in the darkening old world. It introduced a new kind of hero... (1955:5)

Such a hero defined American's separation from Europe and demonstrated national birth.

It explains why post-colonial novelists utilised this genre to define the birth of their new nations and it defined their experiences in relation to colonialism; thus *bildungsroman* was used to signify their national birth—their nationhood. It is the chosen genre of several post-colonial novelists from R.K. Narayan's *Swami and Friends* (1935) to Chinua Achebe's *Things Fall Apart* to Salman Rushdie's *The Satanic Verses.* R.K. Narayan is the earliest writer who is considered 'post-colonial' by contemporary theory. R.K. Narayan published 'growing up' stories just as India was becoming independent from Britain, or becoming 'post-colonial'. These growing up stories, such as *Swami and Friends,* were metaphors for the countries, own coming of age. Nguagi wa Thiong in his novel *Weep Not, Child* depicted indigenous selfhood as the desired condition to aspire to.

Comparison of Rudyard Kipling's *Kim* and Mark Twain's *The Adventures of Huckleberry Finn* with classic works of post-colonial literature, such as R.K. Narayan's *Swami and Friends,* Ngugi wa Thiong's *Weep Not, Child* and by extending the comparison to other works of post-colonial minority and feminist writers, certain shared aspects emerge that undermine the classic differences between post-colonial and non-postcolonial. These characteristics are, quite simply (1) Dismissal of westernised values as expressed in the development of hero or heroine's point of view, (2) Nativising the English language as R.K. Narayan did, or changing it to reflect an indigenous consciousness as Raja Rao did in *Kanthapura* by using it in a language that is not one's own but a consciousness that is one's own. The protagonists of post-colonial novel reject cultural contact situation and choose a particular indigenousness.

Twain's Huck *Finn,* Nguagi's *Njorge*, Kipling's *Kim* and Narayan's *Swami* are all children growing up as new nations are forming. They attend their schools coming in contact with the French or English language, with Christian religion and Western ideals. These child protagonists undertake long or short journeys as in Narayan's *Swami* or *Huck Finn* which leads to child's speculation about his identity, a connection with the land and the quintessential culture of the land. The child turns away from westernisation and moves towards an introspective knowledge of who he or she is within the parent culture. Thus post-colonial *bildungsroman* emerges.

A post-colonial *bildungsroman* writer is not just characterised by his historical or chronogical position, i.e., living and writing in an era after colonisation but metaphorically as a post-colonial by his attitude to the colonising culture, to the coloniser's language and by his growth or journey towards indigenousness.

References

Arnold, Mathew (1925). *Culture and Anarchy*. Ed. William S. Knickerbocker. New York: Macmillan.

Ashcroft, Bill; Griffiths, Gareth; Tiffin, Helen (1989). *The Empire Writes Back : Theory and Practice in Post-colonial Literatures.* London : Routledge.

Bhabha, Homi (1992). Post-colonial criticism. Greenblatt, Stephen; Gunn Giles (eds.) *Redrawing the Boundaries*. New York: Modern Language Association. 437-465.

Booth, Wayne (1988). *The Company We Keep : An Ethics of Fiction.* Berkeley: University of California Press.

Lewis, R.W.B. (1955). *The American Adam: Innocence, Tragedy and Tradition in the Nineteenth Century.* Chicago: University of Chicago.

Needer, Charles (ed.) (1959). *The Autobiography of Mark Twain.* New York: Harper and Row.

Rao, Raja (1967). *Kanthapura.* New York: New Directions.

Swales, Martin (1978). *The German Bildungsroman from Wieland to Hesse.* Princeton: Princeton University Press.

2 Swami: An Indian Schoolboy Fiction

The issues of hybridity and poetics of migration present in much of post-colonial literature, written in English was already a major part of fiction of 'Big three': Mulk Raj Anand, R.K. Narayan and Raja Rao, who all were first published in 1930's. Distinctive in style, all three acted as mediators between Indian and Western Narrative modes.

Out of three, R.K. Narayan was less influenced by Western thought process. He, in his essays, pinpointed the misunderstandings inherent in East-West encounters, denying as being a spiritual sage as perceived by Americans. Western thought process during pre-independence era considered all Indians obsessed with spirituality. Contradictory to his assertions, one can perceive in him (his writings) a latent desire to mould into the role of a writer as conceived by Westerners. This aspect is seen in his novel. *The Guide (1958)*, where the protagonist is transformed into a *guru*, thus explicitly giving expression to elements that had been present subtly, in his writings from the outset.

Narayan's early career was strongly shaped by Graham Greene[1] who not only convinced the publisher Hamish Hamilton to publish his first novel, *Swami and Friends* in

1. Letter from Hamish Hamilton to Narayan, 10 August 1935 (special collections, Mugar Memorial Library, Boston University, No. 737, Box 15), quoted by Ram and Ram, *R.K. Narayan: The Early years*, 9. 154; and a letter from Greene dated 23 August 1935, quoted by Ram and Ram, p. 155.

1935 but also became his mentor deeply involved in the writing process of all his novels. Greene and Hamilton suggested changing the title of *Swami* and also re-christened Narayan, with the consequence that Rasipuram Krishnaswami Narayan Swami became 'R.K. Narayan'. However, if one compares Narayan's acquiescence in this English make over which resulted in the loss of 'Swami' from his own name, the picture that begins to suggest is that of a novelist who was half-willing, atleast to let his identity be trimmed to fit perceptions of the reading sections in England in the 1930's.

Although such reading is subjective, one can see from the outset, Narayan's novels fuse Western and Hindu, more specifically Tamil brahmin elements in varied ways, to produce a fiction which is not only situated in an extremely particular environment, but also succeeds in speaking to an international readership. One can say Narayan's fiction merges registers in an act of cultural brokerage that allows it to cross boundaries without losing a sense of Indian specifics.

This fusion of East and West can be traced in his very first novel, *Swami and Friends*. Narayan's first title for *Swami* was 'Swami the Tate'. The ending of the novel (in which the schoolboy hero obsessed with an imminent cricket match) was much in the trend of the best English school boy, a fiction of the late nineteenth and early twentieth centuries bringing the action to a climax. Swami's friends nickname him 'Tate' after Maurice Tate, the cricketer best known to future generations as Harold Larwood's fast bowling partner on the infamous bodyline tour of Australia in 1932-33, a most important episode in the sporting history of the late colonial period. Narayan's intention of using the first title indicates a certain sort of colonial filiation likely to find favour with English readers. Swami heroworships Tate and his friends are fine with that. Perhaps Greene felt that the original title was too specific, not suitable enough for recognisable sub-genre of English schoolboy fiction. It is surmised that the title 'Swami and Friends' was probably influenced by schoolboy classic fiction of Rudyard Kipling's *Stalky and Co.*

(1899). In such fiction, there used to be links between Christianity, team ethic and the colonial mission. Though by no means the first novel of its kind, *Stalky and Co.* had by this time became a blueprint for such empire fiction, demonstrating the mingling of dynamics of public school and apparently far flung corners of Empire. Such schoolboy fiction reflected on how the schools became a breeding ground for the future custodians of Empire.

One wonders how Swami as a character fits into the mould of English schoolboy fiction. Does he represent an ambivalent 'Empire boy' caught in the middle of stressful relationship of East and West? On the surface, *Swami* appears to be an innocent potrait of the escapades of the protagonist and his friends, but probing deeper. One can sense Narayan's own experiences inherent in the novel as a schoolboy in Madras and Mysore. The petty quarrels of the boys, their rivalries and brawls, skirmishes with their schoolmasters omitting obvious cultural specificity: the incident of cricket match stand as a unifying motif merging various narrative elements providing more specifically colonial inflection.

Swami's ambivalent response to empire makes him the punching bag for depiction of clash of cultures. Although Swami accepts the adult world into which he is being socialised, getting internalised into school's primarily colonial curriculum, seeds of rebellion or alternative ideological position is present in his reaction to fanatical scripture master Mr. Ebenezar's tirade against Hinduism making his 'blood boil'. He challenges Ebenezar and gets punished for his misdemeanour (Ch. 1).

The novel's stance is ambivalent as it is poised between Hindu and Western discursive codes reflected in the Mission School's mixed curriculum, consisting of Tamil and Christian scripture. Swami positions himself as a South Indian, as he takes his Tamil exam, he writes his address on the paper flap:

Tamil Tamil
W.S. Swaminathan

1st Form A Section
Albert Mission School
Malgudi
South India
Asia.

One can defect how Malgudi, South India and Asia are the geographical coordinates provided and how his act of self-positioning occur under the heading 'Tamil'. Narayan never gave a precise reply to questions asked about the location of Malgudi. The universality of the town makes it a symbolic *locus* for exploration of his imaginative pre-occupations. Still one can sense South Indian specificity of Malgudi. Malgudi is more than an anglicised version of South India. It is an imaginary place where the conflicts characterising the social world during the reign of British Empire take place.

R.K. Narayan's stance towards Indian Freedom struggle can be seen in Chapter 12 of *Swami and Friends.* The chapter is titled 'Broken Panes' and it encapsulates a microcosmic juvenile version of the struggle, as the boys shout Gandhian slogans and break window panes on a day of national protest. Narayan makes this incident a part of escapades and pranks of schoolboy genre of fiction diffusing its potential for a serious political statement. However, Swami gets breaten up by the headmaster for his involvement, he runs away saying "I don't care for your dirty school", thus making the incident a strong political statement about the cruelties inflicted during the British Raj. Narayan subverts the British schoolboy fiction conventions by inserting such a provocative incident.

The ending of the novel is dark as Swami runs away, misses the match and the team loses. The game of 'cricket' does not resolve the plot's complications as it might be expected to do in a filiative colonial contribution to the schoolboy fiction genre.

Reference

R.K. Narayan (1985), *Swami and Friends,* Mysore: Indian Thought Publication.

3 Characters in *Swami and Friends*

Characterisation in a work of art is the most important yardstick to judge a writer. A successful artist is recognised not by his story telling, plot construction, etc., but by his craft of creating fascinating characters. Characters need to be well drawn, psychologically penetrating, philosophically bent, then only the novelist is considered excellent. R.K. Narayan's characters, unlike the English novelists', are not of topical or utilitarian value; they are realistic meaning true to life and represent a certain Indian trait in them. Narayan knew that the Indian sensibility is different from the Western, and hence his novels depict a wholly different mentality where godly or demonic characters are easily acceptable; demons, sages, gods and kings do not appear remote concoctions rather become symbols and types stamping out psychological validity.

R.K. Narayan is a realistic writer as he does not potray the qualities of his characters rather he observes how his characters react to their social world, the world in which they perform their daily routine. Swaminathan, a schoolboy, does not like Monday after the delicious leisure of Saturdays and Sundays.

> He shuddered at the very thought of school: that dismal yellow building; the fireeyed Vedanayagam, his class teacher, and the headmaster with his thin long cane...

Narayan aptly draws out the psychology of schoolboy

in these lines indicative of complete grasp of his own boyhood. R.K. Narayan was born in South Indian middle class family. Because of this background he could detect the whims, oddities and eccentricities in South Indian middle class people and represent it in all his novels. He expresses through his novels the way of life of groups of people whose psychology he was most familiar with. He describes Swami's teacher in the words, may be inspired by some sort of prototype he must have come across in his life.

> ... That there was more hair on his chin than one saw from the bench and that he was very very bad looking.

Swami is one of Narayan's Iconic character with whom the novelist reveals the experiences of the days of his own boyhood and youth and they have been transmuted in his early novels deliberately. The protagonists of his later novels; Chandran of *The Bachelor of Arts* and Krishnan of *The English Teacher* are developed forms of Swaminathan whose life may be based on R.K. Narayan's childhood experiences.

Rajeev Taranath regards *Swami and Friends* as a "novel of character on which one could stand on analysis of the use of character and interaction in Narayan's work". The novel starts with the children's world which seems like heaven but in the first two lines the novelist depicts the moods, treatment, behaviour and the child psychology of Swaminathan, the hero of the novel:

> It was Monday Morning, Swaminathan was reluctant to open his eyes. He considered Monday specially unpleasant in the calendar. After the delicious freedom of Saturday and Sunday, it was difficult to get into the Monday mood of work and discipline.

Swaminathan, middle class, average boy becomes friends with his classmates especially with Mani and Rajam with whom he develops good bonding. Mani is described as the mighty good for nothing, the vagabond of the class who

---

* Rajeev Taranath: *The Average As the Positive, op.cit.*, p. 363.

never brought books to class or did homework. The other friend is Rajam, who copies European language and behaviour, speaks good English "Exactly like a European". Apart from Mani and Rajam, Swami has got another set of friends like Somu, Sankar and Samuel. About Samuel the novelist potrays particular details to highlight the possessive qualities of Swaminathan:

> The fourth friend was Samuel known as the "Pea" on account of his size. There was nothing outstanding about him. He was just ordinary, not outstanding virtue of muscle or intellect. He was bad in Arithmetics as Swaminathan was.

This extensive treatment of Samuel in the novel shows how R.K. Narayan is able to make an ordinary character different on virtue of some different traits.

Swaminathan passes through various stages in the novel which shows his school life and changing relationships with his friends. Apart from Swami trying to appear Rajam in every way, the story hurriedly moves towards the destructive demonstration of Swami's quiet life as he joins anti-school processions, breaks the ventilator of the Headmaster's room, and enjoys himself running beresk in the procession. He gets punished for this act which makes him cross the frontiers of boyhood. He leaves the school:

> He restrained the tears that were threatening to rush out... grasping his books, rushed out muttering, 'I do not care for your dirty school'.

He gets admitted to Board High School (a new school, new mates, different environment), but here, too, he does not like studies as he gets bored with no action. He ultimately exhibits the same behaviour what he did with Albert Mission School's Headmaster and at last gets expelled. After this expulsion, he is supposed to play for Malgudi Cricket Club (M.C.C.), but he never plays. He wanders around anticipating the hero's exile and wanderings, Narayan's recurring motif in most of his novels. He returns home finally pacifying the palpitating heart of Granny, mother and father.

Swami is not like other children. His activities show distinctive trait in him which makes him different from other children. His denunciation of Ebenezar, the Bible teacher is provoking; his challenging the teacher shows that he has a mind to grasp things, even question them. His love for his native land is noteworthy, though comic. His devotion to Malgudi Cricket Club (M.C.C.) touches chord of every cricket-loving young boy.

The adult characters in the novel are minor in aspect, but they do complement Swami's evolution as a character. Granny, the school Headmaster, and the teachers particularly the scripture teacher, Ebenezar and the Arithmetic teacher Vedanyagam are characters of substance, though getting not much space. These characters have been exaggerated as they have been viewed through the eyes of a child. However, their relevance is a must to highlight Swami's traits.

In Raja Rao and M.R. Anand, the characters are charged with the love for country and inspired by Gandhian philosophy do appear and play a vital role; however, in Narayan the trace is rather suggestive not dealt in detail. One feels that Narayan is conscious of country's problems, he is hostile towards the British tyranny, yet he cannot totally depict it in his novel about children. In case of Swaminathan, the extraordinary activities do not last long as normalcy is again restored after Rajam leaves.

Thus, one can perceive in *Swami and Friends* subtle characterisation by R.K. Narayan making the novel a juvenile classic.

Reference

R.K. Narayan (1985). *Swami and Friends,* Mysore: Indian Thought Publications.

4 Realism in R.K. Narayan's Novels

The fictional world of R.K. Narayan appears to be the mirror image of the actual world which we live in. His novels do not depict fashionable modes of fiction writing, or themes of eye-catching topicality. In most of his novels, he reflects on the matters of ordinary everyday life. Being an intrinsic part of the national life, his novels are universal in every sense.

Realism means depiction of things as they really are, or as they appear to be; it also signifies the art of making the unreal appear as real. For some scholars, realism is the fidelity observed in the transcription of life, whereas to some others it is plausible interpretation of life.

R.K. Narayan does not deal with photographic reality, he shows reality which is artistic. This differentiates him from the French realist writers, who potrayed stark naked reality in their novels. Narayan does not just report realistic situations; he reflects the Indian mind fully with all its gullibility, superstitious comprehension of life, and its puzzling contradictions. The technique of comic irony can be detected in his novels. How far Narayan is realistic in the manner of his narration can be seen from the harmony which his narration acquires in the blending of theme and the style.

Narayan's novels do not go beyond their middle class milieu. His style is not colourful or sensational. Narayan's simple diction keeps up with the daily rhythm of life of the middle class people of Malgudi. According to Philip Rahv:

> ...All that we can legitimately ask of a novelist in the matter of language is that it must be appropriate to the matter in hand. What is social must not stand in a contradictory relation to the way it is said...

He draws out the common rhythm of Indian life. His art can be compared to Ben Jonson or Charles Dickens, who dealt with oddities and eccentricities of individuals, their incompatibilities rather than the human predicament.

Malgudi, the fictional town of his novels, depicts in microcosmic level of the whole India. This town can be compared to Thomas Hardy's Wessex and it symbolises Indian reality. Malgudi embodies structural solidity of Indian reality pervaded by the customs and traditions, which frame human identity and its *spatio-temporal continuum.* Serious and Comic elements are juxtaposed in his novels within the framework of realistic encounters. The typical India is represented in all his novels. His novels show the interaction of characters and typical Indian situations.

Basically, the stories about Indian life, his novels potray individuals who are deeply connected to Indian social order. Indian reality in his novels is reflected in the perpetual clash between tradition and modernity. "Malgudi", observes Prof C.D. Narasimhiah, "is the microcosm of traditional Indian Society". Whatever takes place in Malgudi, happens through all over India with regional shifts and nuances. Events are not restricted to local, social, or political issues but depict the changing socio-cultural and socio-political influences which affect the day-to-day life of a typical Indian. Narayan's protagonists are human types and their problems are universal problems. Malgudi's case is reflective of the, 'nation's case'.

It is quite apparent from *Swami and Friends* that there is hardly any 'ragging' in our schools, and the dreadful tyrants are not bullies of Tom Brown's school days but headmasters and teachers. Ebenezer's denunciations of Krishna was the standard teaching in Missionary Schools of pre-independence era. The chapter on Broken Panes, which talks about a strike in the school on the occasion of the Non-cooperation Movement, has a historical as well as an intrinsic interest. The different experiences of Swami, the hero, and his friends Mani and Rajam at Albert Mission School, have been realistically rendered. The final chapter of the novel presents the sad fact of separation, but scenes in the school are full of rollicking humour, very natural and true to life-delineating a lively picture of Indian schools.

The image of India which Narayan delienates in his novels has a universality of vision. *The Times Literary Supplement* states: What is true of Malgudi is true in the whole world. "Malgudi is an image of India and a metaphor of everywhere else," observes Prof William Walsh. For Cynthia Vanden Drieson about the Indian colouring of Narayan's novels, there is a presence of universal human nature.

Despite all the universal acclaim, Narayan "does not dwell upon the garish and the bizarre features on which Naipaul and Nirad C. Choudhury seem to thrive."

Narayan depicts Indian reality in all its simplicity, there are no metaphysical undertones as Raja Rao's novels are set in such ambiguity. His fictional representation of Indian reality is richly human as that of Charles Dickens, but no traces of caricature are detected.

Thus, one can perceive how the novelist is humorously obsessed with the socio-comic aspect of Indian reality, which accounts for the immense readability of his novels.

References

Drieson, Cynthiavanden. "The Achievement of R.K. Narayan". *Lit. East and West,* Vol. XXI, Nos. 1-4 (Austin: Texas Press), 61 print.

Narasimhaiah, C.D. *The Swan and the Eagle* (Simla: Indian Institute of Advanced Study, 1969), p. 136.

Philip, D.S. *Perceiving Indian through the works of Nirad Choudhuri, R.K. Narayan and Ved Mehta* (New Delhi: Sterling, 1986), p. 97.

Rahv, Philip. *Fiction and the Criticism.* (New York: n.p., 1965), p. 58.

Thwaite, Anthony. "The Painter of Signs", in *Times Literary Supplement,* Jan. 20, 1976, pp. 6-7.

Walsh, William. *R.K. Narayan: A Critical Appreciation* (New Delhi: Allied Publishers, 1983), p. 167.

5 Tradition and Modernity in *The Guide*

R.K. Narayan's novels deal with the life of average middle class man. He perceives common life with a sense of realistic humour. He uses the technique of irony to expose middle class hypocrisy. As a writer, he notices small things of life with curious interest. He is a detached observer of everyday life. *The Guide* is one of Narayan's most popular work and is narrated in a series of flashbacks. In this novel, Raju narrates his past and reinterprets his feelings which arise out of memory. The flashback technique is brilliantly executed in the novel. The reminiscences of Raju bring out novel's realistic aspect. The flashback technique arouses the curiosity of the reader. It also reveals Narayan's skills as a born story teller.

The story of *The Guide* moves along a bewildering succession of time shifts. Narayan was deeply involved with people of South Indian film industry, so he borrowed cinematic techniques of jump out, flashback, flash forward and montage. The novel does not follow single cohesive curve from the beginning through the middle to the end. It does not follow the linear development pattern. Thus, the novel has an episodic structure which makes it quite unconventional in terms of narrative technique. The plot of *The Guide* circles freely in time and space, both within and between chapters, moving from the past to the present and back again, and from Malgudi to the Memphi Hills to Mangal in a seemingly random way.

The Guide can be divided into two parts; the first part narrates Raju's childhood, love affair, imprisonment, and the second part exclusively deals with Raju's conversion into a *swami*. Raju's past happens in Malgudi and his present is set in Swami Mangla. There are different narrative voices which separate Raju's past from present. The past is recollected by Raju himself and the present is narrated by the author. As it is well known about R.K. Narayan's specific interest in common people's lives, his plot of *The Guide* also talks about a common man. The novel deals with Raju's love life, his greed for money, his sins and repentance. This novel chronicles the story of a common man's growth from ordinary to extraordinary, from a tourist guide to the spiritual guide. Narayan carefully blends comic and serious, real and fantastic elements in the novel.

Narayan's novels are well known for negotiating traditional with modern. Malgudi, in that sense, becomes a site where various possibilities and positions are tried and tested. *The Guide* is a tale of modern India, though it explores the nature of an ancient Indian institution, that of the *guru*, which does not have any Western counterpart. R.K. Narayan utilises the English word 'Guide' for a more serious message, though the word is used in a lighter vein during conversations. Narayan never uses ornate or excessive descriptions. His words are like pen-pictures which bring reality to the mind of the reader. Narayan is able to handle English language as an immensely flexible tool that conveys both the specific as well as symbolic and the universal. He evokes a quite and subdued atmosphere for his novel. In this novel, Narayan uses multiple narrative techniques like flashback, common idioms/proverbs, comic elements, daily language and double perspective. Thus, the finished product (text) emerges out as interesting, stimulating and provocative.

Narayan uses the imagery and symbolism in the novel which represents India and its culture besides relating universally. Towards the end of the story when Raju is drowning his eyes engrossed towards the mountains, a brilliant sun rises and villagers are the onlookers. By using the technique of juxtaposition the simple background of the

Indian village at sunrise is seen along with the suicide, Narayan effectively conveys the sense of hope with Raju's death, thus, confirming the Indian belief in death and rebirth.

The clash of tradition and modernity is felt through the characters outlook and behaviour. Rosie, Velan, Raju's mother and uncle Gaffur, the driver, Joseph, the steward of the bungalow where Marco stayed, all represent the traditional Indian culture, whereas Raju and Marco exhibit Western or Modern manners and culture. Some situations or incidents in the novel also depict this conflict. It was tradition among the villagers to bow low and touch the feet of elders and venerable persons (Hindus call it '*pranam*'). But Raju after his release from the prison, sitting alone on the river steps, does not allow Velan to do so. "Velan rose, bowed low and tried to touch Raju's feet. Raju recoiled at the attempt 'I'll not permit anyone to do this. God alone is entitled to such a prostration. He will destroy us if we attempt to usurp his rights' "

The novel depicts the conflict of East and West and the assimilation of both as represented by Rosie's transformation into Nalini. Narayan follows Mulk Raj Anand's perception of a journey towards the West in order to come back to the East. From the social viewpoint, *The Guide* shows the Indian society, its rituals, customs, culture, superstitions and religious belief, but also clash of modern and traditional values as symbolised by Raju's mother and his maternal uncle on the one hand and Raju and Rosie on the other. When Marco leaves Rosie, she comes to Raju's house for shelter. Raju's mother is shocked to find her coming alone. She asks, "Who has come with you, Rosie?' Rosie blushed, hesitated and looked at me. I moved a couple of steps backward in order that she might see me dimly and not in all raggedness. I replied, 'I think she has come alone, mother'. My mother was amazed, 'Girls today! How courageous you are! In our day we wouldn't go to the street corner without an escort. And I have been to the market only once in my life, when Raju's father was alive". Raju's mother symbolises traditional Hindu values which deny public exposure to women. A Hindu woman was not supposed to go out alone without a male escort. Whereas Rosie is a modern woman who is not scared to go alone as she is influenced by Western culture. In such a conflict, tradition has to give way to modernity, old values are replaced by new. Raju's mother and his maternal uncle have to leave their home for Raju and Rosie.

The village Mangal in the novel depicts South Indian conventional society, totally conservative in its outlook and behaviour patterns. Although, Western culture has made inroads in the village still castes and traditional occupations continue to exist. Arranged marriages are still part of village household. Astrology is still believed in, washing the feet before a temple visit or pulling the temple chariot along the streets on festive days, reciting sacred verses, consulting an astrologer for auspicious time, etc., are some of the traditional rituals still followed in the village. Raju's fasting to appease the rain gods and bring rain to save the people is the most relevant ritual in the novel. Villagers had clear concept about fasting ritual, it is seen through the character of Velan, "Valan gave a very clear account of what the saviour was expected to do—stand in knee deep water, look to the skies and utter the prayer line for two weeks completely fasting during the period—and to, the rains would come down, provided the man who performed it was a pure soul, was a great Soul". The presence of both ancient Indian tradition and modern Western values is apparent in the novel.

There are two kinds of narration visible in the novel. The flashback, story told by the hero, Raju himself and the second method, in which the writer tells the story of Raju. In the first method the story originates in the past and comes to the present. In the second method, it starts in the present and goes into the future. Both these methods blend towards the end, when Raju sacrifices his life for the sake of the people of the village.

The first method starts in the retrospective past. Raju after getting released from prison, is sitting in a very melancholy mood. He looks at Velan and the villagers in an absent-minded way. Velan mistakes him for *Swami*, in spite of Raju's repeated reminders to him that he is not *Swami* at all. Raju starts narrating his past in a moment of intense self analysis. He is both symbolically and in real life a guide. He guides people who come to Malgudi to their destinations. He is young, helpful, born optimist and always cheerful. He has a small shop on the railway platform of Malgudi. Everyone admired his resourcefulness. He is quite sociable. Everybody likes him. He helped everybody, whoever sought his help. Raju's life changes completely with the entrance of Rosie. One day Marco Polo and Rosie get down at Malgudi station. Marco Polo is described as a famous archaeologist. His purpose in coming to Malgudi was to make a historical study of the Caves of Malgudi. Rosie is his charming wife. Raju initially shows them the caves. Rosie feels frustrated with Marco as he does not pay her any attention and is against the idea of her dancing on public stage. Gradually, she comes closer to Raju. Rosie and Raju start living together as he becomes her dance manager fixing her dance programmes and managing her finances. But quite shockingly, he gets arrested on the charges of forgery. The complaint is made by Marco Polo. Raju goes to Jail and Rosie goes back to Marco Polo. This is the end of Raju's first story upto this point, he tells the story to Velan. It is the flashback technique.

In the present, Raju is uncertain about his future course of action. This is the second part of the narration. It is narrated by the author himself. Velan considers him as a *Swami*. So Raju's role as a *Swamiji* is narrated in this part. Raju becomes very popular and becomes a sort of prophet. After sometime, there is a famine in the village resulting in loss of lives. Raju is asked to rescue the village. His moral sense awakens and he decides to sacrifice his life for the village. After three days, rains come. There is a flood in the river Sarayu and Raju fells down in the river. Thus, the novel ends with Raju actually becoming the real saviour of villagers.

Socially, the novel brings out the transition in India from an old fashioned way of life to modern and urbanised one.

Despite being so aware of the dangers of shamming such a serious thing as being a *guru*, Narayan actually comes out in favour of the institution in the end. He never shows villagers rejecting Raju, or Velan abusing and exposing him. He does not project the novel as propaganda against superstitious villagers and fakes. *The Guide* is not an expose of phoney godmen manipulating the gullible masses.

Narayan did not support tradition in a loud or sententious manner. He never rejects or condemns it but rather creates a space for it. He, in fact, proves it in the novel that in the struggle between tradition and modernity, tradition wins though in a reluctant manner. Raju's sacrifice and repentance were genuine, no matter how painfully flawed his motives might have been earlier, or how ineffectual their outcome. As Paranjape says, "In other words, the irony strengthens the "Hindu" world view, not weakens it, though at first it appears as if the opposite is the case".

References

Paranjape, Makarand (2003), "The Reluctant Guru": R.K. Narayan and *"The Guide". South Asian Review.* 24.2, pp. 170-186.

Narayan, R.K. (2006). *The Guide: A Novel,* n.p.: Penguin.

6 *The Guide:* A Hindu Novel

In the novel, *The Guide,* Narayan shows special fascination for *Swamies* and Saints, *gurus* and guides, charlatans and philistines in India's diverse culture. He uses his characteristic humour to capture the spectrum of Indian life, with its hypocrisies and whims, its superstitions and beliefs, its rigidities and flexibilities. The action of the novel presents two different aspects of Indian culture. Malgudi, a miniature of India, represents the rich traditions of classical culture reflected in dances of Rosie-Nalini and marvellous paintings that embellish Marco Polo's *The Cultural History of South India*. Mangal, the neighbour town village symbolises the spiritual dimension of Indian culture, depicted through Raju's transformation into a celebrated *Swami.* "Thus Raju, Rosie and Marco Polo become temporal symbols of Indian cultural ethos" (Goyal, 143). Marco Polo aspires in unearthing the buried treasures of India's rich cultural past, whereas Rosie seeks satisfaction in the creative channels of classical dancing in the midst of an ever present, live audience. According to Bhagwat S. Goyal, "While Marco is cultural historian of the past, Rosie is a cultural ambassador of the present, and Raju is a cultural prophet of the Future". Raju always had a dream of an elusive future till the time comes when he becomes irrevocably committed to a definite future by undertaking a fast to appease the rain-god. Thus, Past, Present and Future are shown interlinked through these three characters in the novel.

Many aspects of Hindu epics and *puranas* are depicted in the novel. By making the hero a rogue, Narayan adds a touch of folk tale, too. Krishna Sen is of the opinion that the novel starts with idyllic opening scene, then moves on to dramatic dialogue format, layered narrative, multilateral structure compressing time shifts and interwoven digressions, and the final penance for a divine boon to save humanity. Narayan parodies or ironically subverts some aspects by shifting things from mythic past to the imperfect present, such as the *guru* always superior to disciple, or the dialogue about spiritual illumination. Another pattern which is parodied is the Hindu belief in the four stages of the ideal life—student, householder, recluse and ascetic *(bramacharya, garhasthya, vanaprastha* and *sanyasa).* This pattern is totally subverted through the potrayal of protagonist Raju. Raju is a 'student' preparing for life in the Malgudi platform, a 'house holder' and man of affairs in his illegal relationship with Rosie and as her dubious business manager, a 'recluse' during his prison days, and an 'ascetic' in his fake *Swami* persona. Raju's fasting to appease the rain-god reminds one of the story of sage-king Bhagirath who undertook severe penance to bring down the goddess Ganga. However, Raju's sacrifice seems more of a subversion of the Hindu myth.

Thus, the entire ritual by Raju is able to bring peace to famine torn Mangal, although how much instrumental was it in bringing the rain can be a point of dispute.

The Guide can be considered as an ambiguous Hindu novel as Krishna Sen aptly encapsulates the novel's spirit, "The denouement is neither a rejection nor a defense of the Hindu faith—it gestures towards the complexity of life, in which there are no simple solutions. It is this ambiguous and open-ended denouement that raises the novel far above the level of a mere moral Fable, or a story with a simplistic happy ending".

References

Goyal, Bhagwats (1981). "From Picaro to Pilgrim: A Perspective on R.K. Narayan's "The Guide"—*Indo-English Literature.* Ed. K.K. Sharma, Ghaziabad: Vimal Prakashan, pp. 127-135.

Sen, Krishna (2004). *Critical Essays on R.K. Narayan's The Guide: With an Introduction to Narayan's Novels.* Kolkata: Orient Longman Pvt. Ltd.

This page left blank

7 The Ending of *The Guide*

The ending of the novel *The Guide* leaves a reader with so many unanswered questions. Who is Raju in the end? Is he a real saint or is he a fake? This question has intrigued all the readers of the novel since its publication. Sally Appleton in her review titled "The Ambiguous Man", observes:

> "The author must decide whether or not holiness will work... the author abandons the reader to choose arbitrarily whether or not, as Raju sinks into the muddy river bed, he is dying, whether or not, as the water rises to Raju's knees, it rises because "it is raining in the hills" or because Raju himself is sagging into it (cited in Pontes and Ezekiel 92)", (quoted in Paranjape, 176).
>
> Critics have varied opinion regarding Raju in the end. G.S. Balarama Gupta feels that Raju in the end seems more of a selfish swindler, an adroit actor, and a perfidious, megalomaniac, whereas C.D. Narasimhaiah puts Raju into the category of a saint, a changed man towards the end (Paranjape, 177).

The question arises if Narayan intended us to perceive Raju as a Fake, then he was not only questioning one individual but an institution of *Guru* itself. So the real issue is not that Raju is a willing saint or not, or that he is unfit for *gurudom*. The people of Mangal believed that it would rain and thus put an end to the drought if a true *Sanyasi* did genuine fasting for twelve days. Hindus believed in such rituals whether they experienced it or not, they never lost their faith in it. Narayan was only depicting those beliefs and rites. He never glorified or condemned such faith. It is not specified whether it rained or not in the novel. Rather one can doubt it based on the description of the topography. The last paragraph of the novel is as follows:

> He got up on feet. He had to be held by Velan and another on each side. In the profoundest silence the crowd followed at a solemn silent pace. The eastern sky was red. Many in the camp were still sleeping. Raju could not walk, but, he insisted upon pulling himself along the same. He panted with the effort. He went down the steps of the river, halting for breath on each step, and finally reached the basin of water. He stepped into it, shut his eyes, and turned towards the mountain, his lips muttering the prayer. Velan and another held him each by an arm. The morning sun was out now; a great shaft of light illuminated the surroundings. It was difficult to hold Raju on his feet, as he had a tendency to flop down. They held him as if he were a baby. Raju opened his eyes, looked about and said, 'Velan, it's raining in the hills. I can feel it coming up under my feet, up my legs.' He sagged down.

There is a contradiction in the natural descriptions as eastern sky being red and the apparition of the morning sun and the great shaft of light illuminating the surroundings do not match with rain in the hills. The readers are left with series of ambiguous questions. Does it really rain? Does Raju survive to see the miracle? Does he die deluded? The readers have to fit the missing pieces into this puzzle. As Makarand Paranjape says, "Are we people of faith, those who believe that the sacrifice of a well intentioned individual can solve social problems, even change the course of natural events? Or are we modern, "Scientific" people who refuse to yield to such superstitions? To frame the choices offered by the novel in an even more complex manner, do we want to believe even though we might be unable to?".

Thus, Raju although a fake *guru* seemed to grow in stature as the novel progresses. He willingly sacrifices his life. Raju knew that he could not change people's misconceptions about him. They felt that he was a true *Sanyasi* and hence his fast would bring rain. He was trapped. He could have saved himself as the doctors and Velan requested him to stop fasting. But if he had stopped fasting what thousands of people would think about him? Would not it be a betrayal of faith laid on him by the people? So, he considers it a better option to die a martyr's life rather than be hated by people. Narayan somehow tells the readers that Raju is present with his positives and negatives in each of us.

References

Paranjape, Makarand (2003). "The Reluctant Guru": R.K. Narayan and *The Guide. South Asian Review.* 24.2. pp. 170-186.

Narayan, R.K. (2006). *The Guide: A Novel,* n.p.: Penguin.

This page left blank

8 Velan's Character in *The Guide*

The peripheral character who is crucial to the development of the plot is Velan. His character is not drawn in detail, nor is it required. Velan does not seem to fit into Western setting. Velan is the sole person in the whole novel who is responsible for Raju's final fate. But Velan's role is not only to oppress Raju. It is Velan who makes Raju a "saint", and it is Velan's unshakable faith that makes Raju rise above himself. Velan can be considered sort of catalyst for Raju's apotheosis.

Velan is symbolic of psychological reality of the rural setting. He is the real spiritual guide of Raju who is the professional guide of the novel. According to U.P. Singha from his essay, "Patterns of myth and Reality in "The Guide": Complex craft of fiction":

> Their (Raju, Velan and Rosie) implicative or metaphoric roles in the novel make a mythic triangle which is a triangle with three points, one indicating the height of spiritual-cum-moral triumph. The point indicating the law, the deep is represented by Rosie, and the vertical one is represented by Velan. The third point at the level, which seems to be vertical but is not obviously so, represents Raju. The first two points act upon this one so that the whole triangle becomes mythical-man facing two opposite worlds; facing always with very little chance of a smooth and painless arrival here or there.

Thus, Velan's character is important as he is the medium who connects the real world Raju to the spiritual world *Swami* Raju. What if he had not met Velan, then we would not have a character like Raju, who is eventually cleansed of all sins and flaws. Velan also speeds up the narrative as he acts on behalf of the readers as an audience. He fulfills the requirements of an ideal story telling situation. He is as essential for the narrative as the main character themselves.

Reference

Singha, U.P. (1988). "Patterns of Myth and Reality in "The Guide": Complex Craft of Fiction". *Patterns of Myth and Reality: A Study in R.K. Narayan's Novels*. By U.P. Singha. Delhi: Sandarbh Publishers, pp. 70-94.

9 Works Cited

Chapter 1

1. Arnold, Matthew. *Culture and Anarchy,* Ed. William S. Knickerbocker. New York: Macmillan, 1925.
2. Ashcroft, Bill; Griffiths, Gareth; Tiffin, Helen. *The Empire Writes back: Theory and Practice in Postcolonial Literature.* London: Routledge, 1989.
3. Bhabha, Homi. Postcolonial Criticism. Greenblatt, Stephen; Gunn Giles; eds. *Redrawing the Boundaries.* New York: Modern Language Association, 1992, pp. 437-465.
4. Booth, Wayne. *The Company We Keep: An Ethics of Fiction.* Berkeley: University of California Press, 1928.
5. Lewis, R.W.B. *The American Adam: Innocence, Tragedy and Tradition in the Nineteenth Century.* Chicago: University of Chicago, 1955.
6. Needer, Charles; eds. *The Autobiography of Mark Twain.* New York: Harper and Row, 1959.
7. Rao, Raja. *Kanthapura.* New York: New Directions, 1967.
8. Swales, Martin. *The German Bildungsroman from Wieland to Hesse.* Princeton: Princeton University Press, 1978.

Chapter 2

1. Hamilton, Hamish. *Special Collections.* Boston University Press, 1935, p. 737.
2. Narayan, R.K. *Swami and Friends.* Mysore: Indian Thought Publication, 1985.

Chapter 3

1. Narayan, R.K. *Swami and Friends.* Mysore: Indian Thought Publications, 1985.
2. Taranath, Rajeev. *The Average as the Positive.* n.p.: n.p., N.D. 363.

Chapter 4

1. Drieson, Cynthiavanden. "The Achievement of R.K. Narayan". *Lit. East and West.* Vol. XXI (N.D.): 1-4. Austin: Texas Press. 61. Print.
2. Narasimhaiah, C.D. *The Swan and the Eagle.* Simla: Indian Institute of Advanced Study, 1969, p. 136.
3. Philip, D.S. *Perceiving Indian Through the Works of Nirad Chaudhuri, R.K. Narayan and Ved Mehta.* New Delhi: Sterling, 1986, p. 97.
4. Rahv, Philip. *Fiction and the Criticism.* New York: n.p., 1965, p. 58.
5. Thwaite, Anthony. "The Painter of Signs", in *Times Literary Supplement* (Jan. 20): pp. 6-7. Print.
6. Walsh, William. *R.K. Narayan: A Critical Appreciation.* New Delhi: Allied Publishers, 1983, p. 167.

Chapter 5 to 8

1. Goyal, Bhagwat S. "From Picaro to Pilgrim: A Perspective on R.K. Narayan's The Guide". *Indo-English Literature.* Ed. K.K. Sharma. Ghaziabad: Vimal Prakashan, 1981, pp. 127-135.
2. Kumar, Gajendra. "R.K. Narayan's 'The Guide': A Search for Socio-Cultural Crisis". *Indian English*

Literature: A New Perspective. New Delhi: Sarup and Sons, 2001, pp. 25-33.

3. Mathur, O.P. "The Guide: A Study in Cultural Ambivalence". *The Modern Indian English Fiction.* Ed. O.P. Mathur. New Delhi: Abhinav Publications, 1993, pp. 89-97.

4. M.K. Naik. Madras: The Macmillan Company of India Ltd., 1979, pp. 172-198.

5. Nair, Rama. "Gunas as Determinants of Character: A Study of R.K. Narayan's. *The Guide*". *Osmania Journal of English Studies,* 26 (1990). 41-48, Print.

6. Narasimhaiah, C.D. "R.K. Narayan's *The Guide*". *Aspects of Indian Writing in English,* 2006.

7. Paranjape, Makarand. "The Reluctant Guru": R.K. Narayan and *The Guide*". *South Asian Review,* 24.2 (2003): 170-186, Print.

8. Perry, John Oliver. "Irresolvable Bi-cultural Conflicts and Other Ironies in Narayan's *The Guide". Recent Commonwealth Literature:* Vol. 1. Eds. R.K. Dhawan, P.V. Dhamija and A.K. Shrivastava. New Delhi: Prestige Books, 1989, pp. 170-180.

9. Rani, T. Asoka. "Chinua Achebe's *Arrow of God* and R.K. Narayan's *The Guide*: A study on the Ritualistic Foundations of Society". *The Literary Half Yearly,* 36.1 (1995). 61-69. Print.

10. Sankaran, Chitra. "Patterns of Story telling in R.K. Narayan's *The Guide. The Journal of Commonwealth Literature,* 26.1 (1991). 127-150. Print.

11. Sen, Krishna. *Critical Essays on R.K. Narayan's The Guide: With an Introduction to Narayan's Novels.* Kolkata: Orient Longman Pvt. Ltd., 2004.

12. Singha, U.P. "Patterns of Myth and Reality in "The Guide": Complex Craft of Fiction". *Patterns of Myth and Reality: A Study in R.K. Narayan's Novels.* By U.P. Singha. Delhi: Sandarbh Publishers, 1988, pp. 70-94.

13. Soule, Arun. "The Evolution of *The Guide*: The Individual-Society Equation in the Indian and the Western Contexts." *Indian Writing in English: Perspectives.* Ed. Jaya Chakravarty. New Delhi: Atlantic Publishers and Distributors, 2003, pp. 29-33.

14. Sundaram, P.S. "The Guide". *R.K. Narayan as a Novelist.* By P.S. Sundaram. Delhi: B.R. Publishing Corporation, 1988, pp. 73-82.

15. Yadav, B.S. "The Guide—A Psycho-philosophic and Social Ethical Study." *Indian Writings in English.* Vol. 4. Ed. Manohar K. Bhatnagar. New Delhi: Atlantic Publisher and Distributor, 1999, pp. 24-28.

Reference

Narayan, R.K. *The Guide: A Novel.* n.p.: Penguin, 2006.